Get Around in the City

5-99

Get Around

in the City

Get Around in the City

by Lee Sullivan Hill

Carolrhoda Books, Inc./Minneapolis

For my car-crazy sister Judy, with love.
—L. S. H.

For more information about the photographs in this book, see the Photo Index on pages 30–32.

The photographs in this book are reproduced through the courtesy of: © Junebug Clark/Photo Researchers, Inc., cover; © Richard Cummins, pp. 1, 8; © Will & Deni McIntyre/Photo Researchers, Inc., p. 2; © Sophie Dauwe/Robert Fried Photography, pp. 5, 10; © Buddy Mays/Travel Stock, pp. 6, 22, 28; © Jeff Isaac Greenberg/Photo Researchers, Inc., p. 7; © Betty Crowell, p. 9; © Howard Ande, pp. 11, 29; © Alyx Kellington/DDB Stock Photography, p. 12; © Tony Stone Images/ Frank Cezus, p. 13; © Tony Stone Images/Don Smetzer, p. 14; © David Weintraub/Photo Researchers, Inc., p. 15; © Rafael Macia/Photo Researchers, Inc., pp. 16, 21, 25; © Tony Stone Images/David H. Endersbee, p. 17; © Don Eastman, p. 18; © Steven Ferry, p. 19; © Stephen Saks/Photo Researchers, Inc., p. 20; © Robert Fried/Robert Fried Photography, pp. 23, 24, 27; © Priscilla Eastman, p. 26.

Carolrhoda Books, Inc., c/o The Lerner Publishing Group
241 First Avenue North, Minneapolis, MN 55401 U.S.A.

Website address: www.lernerbooks.com

Library of Congress Cataloging-in-Publication Data

Hill, Lee Sullivan, 1958–
    Get around in the city / by Lee Sullivan Hill.
       p.   cm. — (A Get around book)
    Includes index.
    Summary: An introduction to some of the different ways people get around in cities, from walking and biking to ferryboats and skates.
    ISBN 1-57505-307-1
    1. Urban transportation—Juvenile literature.
    [1. Transportation. 2. City and town life.] I. Title.
    II. Series: Hill, Lee Sullivan, 1958–   Get around book.
    HE305.H348   1999
    388.4—dc21   98-25000

Manufactured in the United States of America
1 2 3 4 5 6 – JR – 04 03 02 01 00 99

Zoom-boom, beep-beep. Get around in the city.
Transportation takes you where you want to go.

In a city full of people, there are many ways to get around. Do you want to go by car?

There are big cars, small cars, old and new. Taxicabs and trucks and vans. What a traffic jam!

Get around on foot. You might get there faster. City buildings are close together. You can walk from store to store.

Some streets are closed to cars and open to people.
Crowds of walkers flow like rivers.

Crowds of bike riders get around, too. Some cities have roadways just for bikes.

Others have bike paths in the park. Ride by yourself or with a friend. Bikes are a kind of transportation you use on your own.

Some kinds of transportation are made to share. Buses roll from stop to stop. You can catch a bus to get uptown.

Climb the steep stairs of a double-decker bus.
The world looks different from way up there.

Some shared transportation runs on rails. Take the A train in New York . . . the El in Chicago . . . or the T in Boston. It's a transportation alphabet!

In San Francisco, cable cars ride on rails in the middle of the street. Underground cables move the cars up and down steep hills.

In cities near the water, you can get around by boat.
Ferryboats in New York City carry groups of people
across the harbor.

Everyone uses boats in Venice, Italy. The city was built on islands. Taxi boats and gondolas glide up and down canals.

People in some cities use animals for transportation.
How would you like to hire an elephant to get around?

Or would you rather ride a motorcycle? Motorcycles don't use much gas. They are easy to park, too.

Some city workers must get around FAST! Firefighters
in shiny engines rush to a fire.

Police cars zoom to the rescue. Sirens blare, lights flash. Everyone get out of the way!

Some people like to go fast for fun. Put on a pair of
skates and a helmet. Skates can take you fast and far!

Other people like to slow down and look around.
Clip-clop down a stone street. It doesn't matter
where you go. The fun part is the ride.

How would you choose to get around in the city?
Going on a field trip? Take a school bus.

In a hurry? Grab a cab.

On a sunny day, you might want to walk.

If it's raining, try the subway. It goes underground.

In cities around the world, people find all kinds of ways to get around.

Day or night, the city never stops moving.

Photo Index

 **Cover** All the vehicles on this street in New York City are headed in the same direction. In many areas, one-way streets flow in alternate directions from one block to the next. This helps traffic move more smoothly.

Page 6 This snazzy sports car is parked on Ocean Avenue in Miami, Florida. Many people use cars for transportation because they are convenient and quick . . . and sometimes beautiful.

 **Page 1** The Metromover carries passengers high above the crowds of Miami, Florida. It is called a monorail because it runs on a single rail. (*Mono* in *monorail* means "one.")

Page 7 This photo of New York City shows an amazing variety of vehicles. Taxicabs carry passengers for a fee, cars weave their way through the traffic, and trucks and vans are on their way to pick up and deliver goods.

 **Page 2** Rickshaw drivers in Bombay, India, pedal paying passengers to places all over the city. Rickshaws take the place of taxicabs in many cities. They look a lot like big tricycles.

Page 8 People enjoy strolling down High Street in Kilkenny, Ireland. People traveling on foot are called pedestrians. With its shops, restaurants, and wide sidewalks, Kilkenny is friendly to pedestrians.

 **Page 5** About 11,000,000 people live in Beijing, China, where this photo was taken. From Beijing to Boston, traffic jams are part of city life. Even though traffic slows down, the busiest parts of the day are called "rush hour."

Page 9 This photo of a crowded street was taken on a Sunday afternoon in Beijing, China. City streets aren't just for motorized vehicles—some are open only to pedestrians. A street set aside for walkers is called a pedestrian mall.

Page 10 Bicycles and cars are separated from each other on this road in Chengdu, China. Barricades keep bicyclists safe from motor vehicles.

Page 15 Even though the cable cars of San Francisco, California, are old, residents keep them running. The cable cars have become a symbol of their city.

Page 11 Bicyclists in Chicago, Illinois, can avoid city traffic by following the bike path along Lake Michigan. Bicycles are a kind of private transportation— the riders own the bikes and choose where and when they want to ride.

Page 16 Millions of people travel across New York Harbor every year on the Staten Island Ferry. Most are commuters, who ride each day from their homes on Staten Island to jobs in Manhattan.

Page 12 A bus makes its way through traffic in Panama City, Panama. Buses, trains, trolleys, subways, and ferryboats are a few kinds of public transportation, which is shared by people in a community.

Page 17 The Grand Canal is one of the main waterways in Venice, Italy. It is so wide that hundreds of boats can gather there. Other canals are so narrow that only one thin gondola can creep along their course.

Page 13 People who live in London, England, ride red double-decker buses to offices and shops and back home again. Tourists ride them just for fun. Narrow steps curve up to the top level of each bus.

Page 18 Elephants are highly valued in Southeast Asia for their great strength. In Jaipur, India, they give rides to tourists. Outside the city, elephants carry cargo, haul lumber, and carve roads through the forest.

Page 14 The El train in Chicago, Illinois, got its name from the word *elevated*. In Boston, a T for *transit* marks bus, trolley, and subway stops. The A train is one line in a vast subway network under the streets of New York City.

Page 19 This motorcycle rider in England carries letters and small packages in his bag. Motorcycles are great for deliveries in the city because they are small and quick.

Page 20 This aerial ladder truck is operated by firefighters in San Francisco, California. It takes two drivers to steer the long truck around corners. One driver sits in front and the other sits in back.

Page 25 These taxicabs are driving through Times Square in New York City. Taking a cab costs more than riding the bus or the subway. But a cab can zip you right to the front door of a Broadway theater to see a show.

Page 21 The New York City Police Department, like most others, uses cars that have been fixed up to help officers do their jobs. The cars have heavy-duty shock absorbers, sirens and lights, and even laptop computers.

Page 26 This woman walks through her neighborhood in Bhaktapur, Nepal. Walking is the oldest form of transportation, and it's still one of the best ways to get around in the city.

Page 22 This young man in Miami, Florida, is skating just for fun. But sometimes in-line skates help people work in the city. Delivery people and office commuters get around on in-line skates, too.

Page 27 This subway train runs underground in Santiago, Chile. Subways are designed to move large numbers of people through a city quickly. Riders avoid bad weather and heavy traffic on city streets.

Page 23 This horse-drawn carriage in Quebec City, Canada, might make you imagine the olden days. Before cars were invented, horses were a major form of transportation.

Page 28 A donkey pulls a homemade cart in Alma-Ata, Kazakhstan. People make use of whatever kind of transportation they can find to get around in the city.

Page 24 This school bus in San Juan, Puerto Rico, is picking up students after a field trip to Old San Juan.

Page 29 Nighttime traffic rolls along on Michigan Avenue, while lights glitter and glow on the stone walls of the Old Water Tower in Chicago, Illinois.